LITANY FOR THE PIG

poems by
Eva Bourke

illustrations by
Jay Murphy

Cover illustration by Miriam Bourke
Typeset and designed by The Copy Bureau, Galway
Printed by Berry's, Westport
Bound by Kenny's Fine Binding

© Eva Bourke, 1989. All rights reserved.
ISBN 0 948 339 23 3 Hardcover £8.50
ISBN 0 948 339 24 1 Softcover £4.95

Produced with the assistance of
The Arts Council
(An Chomhairle Ealaíon)

Salmon Publishing,
Auburn, Upper Fairhill, Galway

for **Ono, Gabriel, Miriam
and Benji**

*"Powerful of the earth, masters of new poisons,
sad secret guardians of final thunder,
the torments heaven sends us are enough.
Before your finger presses down, stop and consider."*
Primo Levi

Contents

Open Heart Surgery	1
The Third Coming	3
Ode To The Lemon	7
Clare	9
Tuscan Dragonfly	11
For D.W.	14
The Centuries Taught Us	15
After The Great Passion	17
Moments Musicaux	19
Enchantment of Snails	25
Inventory	27
The Museum of Conquest	29
Young Bat	33
Litany For The Pig	35
The Elder	39
Chaplin Mimes Mr. Hyde Turning Into Dr. Jekyll	42
Voltaire's Monkeys	44
Sea Escape	47
Diptych Of A Wedding	49
Consolation	51
Orpheus And Eurydice In The Underground	53
Gertrud Kolmar, 1894 - 1943	55
The Aquarium	59
The Book	64
The Breakthrough	66
Day Return, Suffolk, Summer '86	68
The Butcher	70
Pygmalion	72
Mackerel	75
Adolescence	77

Open Heart Surgery
for Michael Gorman

On Eyre Square two clowns perform
open heart surgery.

The patient has two hearts
which they remove to the bystanders' delight.

Then they play soccer
with the bigger one,

a bundle of purple knots and muscles
closed tightly as a fist.

People laugh
as they kick it around in the dust.

The clowns' hats are rimfull
with small coins.

In Middle Street
the ground is a goldmine.

Ruins go for a song to high bidders.
Batallions of starlings

make forays into
undertaker's establishments.

Leaderless and precise
they land on the tip

of a flagstaff
fluttering like angels

on a needle.
Ambulances sweep the streets.

A single sax wails outside
the Shoecare Centre.

Two middle-aged Euro-piranhas
in silver hair and red ties

have made a huge kill today.
Eyes dim like headlights.

The Third Coming

They came from the sky
that had been still as water
and was now in great motion
like a rattling machine

and from the water
that had been moving with life
and became rigid now
and still as ice,

they broke in upon us
from all sides,
their horrible eyepieces
and electronic ears

trained on beds and desks,
children's cots,
rivers, the light, the grass,
and it was not long

before our hands caught fire,
our hair became dust,
and many of us burned to cinders
blazing like tree stumps.

The black air seemed quieter,
but choked us with a nimble activity
we learned to dread
also the sound of steel scraping on steel,

or of a fat thunderous belching
that went on at a distance,
filling our heads
and never stopping.

They had found us at last
in this place
where we believed we could,
in all innocence,

stitch together the hours, days, weeks,
a patchwork quilt of time,
with bright and dark needles,
make it from multi-coloured strips,

saffron or yellow for mornings,
rose and azure for the night,
wrap our children in the soft fabric
of long afternoons

spent in the shadow of trees
whose branches intertwined
to form a roof
over abundant and verdurous fields.

Now the earth has been ripped open
by their frantic search,
the treasures are depleted,
the trees cut down,

and you go naked and hungry,
my children,
your bellies swollen,
your skin ashen.

You can neither speak nor sing
since they have taken
your mouth from you.
This is the worst of their crimes.

Their black aircraft
hangs like a spider
over our heads
in a web of cruelty and deceit.

We must learn to dance,
to pirouette and bow,
to sidestep this mesh.
Dance well, children, to the very last

Ode To The Lemon
for Vincent

Who switched on the light
in this dusky garden?
A hundred bulbs ignite
the branches of the lemon tree.

The lemon dangles from the twig,
a drop of honey gone sour.

The lemon and the bee are kindred
in their ancient yearning for sweetness.

The lemon's family are
the sun, melons, parakeets,
the children of China,
the last letter of the Greek alphabet -
Omega.

Inside the lemon
longi-
tudes
of
ice,
latitudes of fire.

The lemon possesses all the marks of a planet,
poles of thirst and fulfilment,
oceans of truth,

seas of tranquillity,
satellites of bitterness.

Lemon geography:
some benighted countries
have never seen the light
of a single lemon.

Lemons can be dangerous in politics.
Once the goddess Athena was refused
a prize lemon by Paris.
A terrible war followed
in which thousands died.

Oblong pips embedded in the lemon's flesh
were made in its own likeness.

When the lemon was given the pick
of trees, it chose wisely,
a stout thorn bush
with dull leaves.
No painter could have offset
its radiance better.

Lemons allow themselves to be ground, sliced,
grated, squeezed, squashed, quartered and
discarded.

Oh paradoxical lemon,
most honest of allies,
leaving yellow barbs on the tongue.

Clare

The stone never quite cools off here
where it has colonised the peninsulae,
the promontories, the hills,
even during the icy winter months
when the north wind shears the mountainsides
like sheep
uttering its fierce fricatives,
there's a touch, an aura of summer

never quite vanquished, for in the depths
of cuts and clefts,
in narrow chinks
between flat table-sized slabs,
emerging from wind-scooped hollows
and vying with watercress
that covers blackish puddles with green dandruff
for shelter and precious substances,

grass grows all year round,
full of desire,
an obstinate mendicant
searching for crumbs of fecundity
from rock to boulder;
on this barren loom it weaves
the thirsty fibres of its roots
into a soft and enduring fabric.

Near Black Head the landscape

resembles an overcrowded graveyard
and the sea hits out
against the shore
like a penitent
beating his breast in a frenzy,
unaware of the good news
the grass keeps spreading.

In January Siberian winds bundle crows
across a low, grey sky,
chisel the country down to the bones.
But they say you can feel
its warmth if you place your palm
on the stone for a while
and the stirring
of hundreds of very fine blades.

Tuscan Dragonfly

I am libellula, quick dragonfly,
I am impatient, wanton, always hungry.
I hitch hooks into the day.
Those who fear me call me devil's needle.
I sting. I'm a green-blue lightning flash.
Anchoring my screen of attack and retreat
in the flickering heat
I hum the syncopic song of blood sports
above dry grass.
See how well equipped I am,
admire my body, a metallic, slim-waisted
killer's device, my visored face
and compound eyes always on the search
for weaklings, mosquitos, butterflies.
They fill me with contempt,
those honey-eaters,
mesmerized by the perfumes
of broom and lavender.
I give them no peace, skim the pond,
spy, ambush, devour.
I live in the air like a kite
sailing on finely veined cellophane wings.

But my time will come
when I too must touch down
as inscribed on the blueprint of my life.
Drugged by slow juices
that inexplicably run through me,

I sit immobile on the laurel hedge
beneath my mate, a thin brown twig
with stunted wings,
throwing all caution to the wind,
letting come what may.

For D.W.

I would trade any Scala singer's
glacial heights
for the warm sandpaper
of her voice's gladly obeyed commands.
Daughter of ballad singers
and instrument makers
from the Liberties,
in her Ballyfermot back-garden
full of Jerusalem artichokes,
Rhenish vines, Siberian rabbits,
Chinese quail and crowds
of local children.
I slept beside her
in her wide strawberry bed,
felt the rasp of her rough shins
and listened to her heave deep breaths
from her smoke-corroded lungs,
knowing that inside her fifteen stone body
was the delicate girl of fourteen
that grew fat after a night of rape,
putting layer upon protective layer
around her,
until the princess left
and the jester was born.
But she never fooled me -
her body had to grow
to accommodate her generous heart,
and to this day
she walks in beauty
on feet of size three.

The Centuries Taught Us

We don't faint at the sight
of an orchid.
Our cool hands turn it to face
the leopard fleck in its throat,
its stigmata, pollen sac, filaments,
the muggy perfumes it exhales,
an antechamber crawling
with dazed courtiers.

Our spice of life is dosed with care:
pepper ash, saffron twigs,
the hot tastes of eruptions
and tidal waves.
We analyse the virtues of islands.
Restless travels lead us to cross
divisions like mountain ranges
while we carry twice the value of a village
in our pockets.

The centuries taught us
to pronounce 'insurgency, massacre,
shoot-to-kill'
with a certain bewildered grace.
We don't faint at the sight
of volcanoes,
nor do images of flaming bodies
unsettle us.
In our frigid studies we observe

our watches flick away the seconds
like children's lives.

The centuries taught us
what can be gained
from purposeful mastery,
have equipped us with the skill
of neck-iron and whip,
plastic bullet, electrode and gas.
We don't faint at the sight
of sequoia or burnt earth.
We sway in our hammocks
while our team of carriers is kept
well within range.

Coming to an end
we have stripped the world down to its bones,
squeezed dry its arteries
and crumpled it up like an old newspaper.
Scorched and smouldering,
ragged and hungry,
it lies there in the glare of the sun;
how much more of our know-how
can it take before it goes up in fire?

After The Great Passion

Where shall we go
when the great passion's over?

Our chairs have crossed their legs
and meditate by the fireside.

The turbulences are allayed.

Our windows have hauled in
flags and figures of speech
and shuttered themselves.

Will we be moved
by the memory of tenderness?

Our carpet flowers blossom timidly,
our lovebirds have shaken out
and folded their plumage,
our entertainers
are behind the scenes
stripping off their glitter.

What bridges will we cross,
without protest,
with just a modicum of despair?

Our doors are shut like eyelids,
the walls say nothing.

Daylight thins in the corners
of our tended gardens.

Our Salto Mortale has come
full circle.
Stealthily we stretch our muscles
on grey mornings,
caress skin and hair
with nervous compassion.

We go quietly
without fuss or roll of drum
on our walks - you and I -
to the sound of our anxious breathing

setting foot before foot
over level paths
that are lit
by a suspicion of pale dawn.

Moments Musicaux

At seventeen I learnt English with a Southern drawl,
bull-frog, water moccasin,
blues, corn bread, blue grass,
Jefferson, U.S. of America,
allegiance to the flag,
pursuit of happiness.
Nothing could have pleased my father more.
"Learn a living language", he'd say,
"Let the dead bury the dead."

At seventeen, my father, a thin-faced boy, holds a top hat
in his left hand, makes mock bows towards the camera,
beside him under a blossoming tree
mother, father, sisters, brother,
sit upright and stiff around a garden table.
The girls handle their needlework like prayer books,
the grandfather, with white beard
and black Sunday frock-coat, gazes sternly
upon such frivolousness. It is 1916.
My father, more lighthearted
than his surly, irate brother,
who has read the entire history of the papacy
by the age of twelve,
has nothing in mind but music.
Bach, Mozart, Chopin
and above all Schubert.
There's the repetition in the left hand of one note,
a slow beat like a human pulse
in one of the sonatas that enthralls him.

With my father's encouragement I learn
soda fountain, I wanna hold your hand,
Thunderbird, Little Rock, segregation,
nigger-lover, civil rights march.

Exiled to boarding school, laughed at by the others
for his old-fashioned knee-length breeches,
he writes home to his favourite sister:
"I must work harder at my Greek,
only second place. Please, don't tell Father.
Our troops have made another victorious foray
into enemy territory. Hooray!
I am writing this from the infirmary,
having fainted in History.
The Professor made me recite
the whole chapter on the Peloponnesian wars.
At the smallest mistake he'd tell me to sit down
and call me out again the next day.
I could never do it.
I didn't sleep or eat for two weeks.
I miss our swims in the river.
Here we're forbidden to go near it.
You should see how much wider it is than at home,
and how majestically it flows through the town.
I know a lot of the Nocturnes now by heart.
I'll play them for you when I get holidays."

At eighteen he's punished for rowing on the Danube.
At eighteen he is sent to the trenches at Verdun,

small for his age, underweight,
to defend the Fatherland, the beloved Kaiser,
with thousands like him,
dulce et decorum est pro patria mori
hammered into their brains.
He's relieved and eager,
glad to seize this chance
to escape the harsh regime of school.
In the middle of trench warfare,
encircled by heavy barrage,
exhausted, louse-ridden, hungry,
he practises the fingering
of the great Étude de la Revolution,
plays a tribute to enlightened France
on an imaginary keyboard.

At that age I learn new words,
master race, deportation, concentration camp,
final solution,
become aware of the horror
of the dictionary of inhumanity,
but also Rock n' Roll, Maple Leaf Rag,
democracy, human rights.

At nineteen he returns, disillusioned
with honour and Fatherland,
becomes a penniless student, his diet of inflation porridge
floating with mouse droppings.
Triple sonatas, preludes, fugues,
he plays Bach over and over again,

on the organ of the city church
while the Brownshirts are rallying and marching
and flooding the squares of Bayreuth
with the blood of their flags.
Stubbornly anti-fascist from the start,
he quickly becomes 'enemy of state number one',
escapes arrest in the nick of time
to Jerusalem where he teaches Palestinian orphans
German and music, never ceasing to marvel
at the 'delicate organization'
of the Arabic children's ears,
their musicality, their ability
to pick up living languages fast.
There's refuge in music,
but none in official jargon -
he learns English: protectorate,
curfew, licence, displaced person,
British subject, alien.
He prunes orange trees in Haifa, Nazareth,
sometimes plays the raindrop prelude
during the hot season,
trying to make the notes sound like water
trickling down window panes.

I continue learning capitalism, power-bloc,
energy crisis, star wars,
and resistance, social justice,
feminism, Sweet Honey, peace.

Returned but never really at home
he emigrates a second time, as he says,
with my mother to Austria,
spends the rest of his life
teaching two country boys to play Schubert, Chopin, Bach,
collects children from school
to drive them to their distant mountain farms
in his small battered car;
'school bus', the villagers call him.

I wish he could be around still
to monitor the slow and fast movements
of my learning process,
the dead and living words,
some harsh and painful, some kind in a detached way,
the ones I love most passionate and clear
and full of music, impromptus,
songs without words,
moments musicaux.

Enchantment Of The Snails
for Miriam

Not in the cities,
not in the planned squares
of the cities
would you find it

but in well corners,
in wet jungly gardens,
in mouldering lairs
between dandelion and nettle:

the slimy script of their tracks
on the crawler lane,
footprints of lazy
creeping soles.

They obey the rhythm
of your spells,
turn at a wink into four-eyed
dancing cobras

or tigers
dragging purple reels
across the hot wilderness
of your hand

faster than light.
They guzzle time

from head to foot
into their spiralled entrail bag

until blue afternoons
and entire summers
tumble down.
I would still like to live

in colourful houses,
whistle melodies
on coiled flutes,
invited the sky to this show

of mobile homes advancing
at a snail's pace,
sculpted chords of plasma and lime
on a child's palm.

Inventory
for Eoin

How proud I am to be part owner
of this planet!
All the time I am kept busy
surveying my property.

Of the passing clouds
that small dark one is mine
and of its raindrops I own
the biggest and coldest.

Nobody ever disputes my rights
over some thornbushes,
yes, in the hedge near the wasteland
where I delight in my patch

of spilled rubbish and dead grass.
I go down to the beach.
Obediently the sea curls up at my feet.
It must be aware

that I have cultivated one square foot
of its ground over the years.
And look at the result, waves,
and stand apart!

These footprints disappearing
into the mouths of - let's say -

2 or 3 sandworms
definitely belong to me.

I have been known
to be in possession of so much:
blank pages in books
for example,

(so the Chamber of Commerce,
one prophet,
three philosophers
and hundreds of historians tell me)

and the last moments of one hour
many years ago.
They endured the length
of just about 3 or 4 heartbeats.

Whatever else is not mortgaged
or in the hands
of greedy anonymous shareholders
I keep on my person

for constant surveillance:
this bit of water,
those ashes,
that blood and sand,

and this wrinkled and black thing
silently and forever
running away
from my feet.

The Museum of Conquest

I
Towers, battlements,
Sphinx-guarded gates,
but no cities.

Frieze after frieze
of great wars,
soldiers, chariots,
horses
are sinking
into the hard froth
of marble.

Rows of giant kings,
their eyes
turned in
towards black stone.

The royal dead
lie in gaudy burial boxes,
bandaged dust,
their grey segmented bodies
resemble empty chrysalides
of huge insects.

And so it continues.
Everything's petrified,
permanently cast

in the posture of attack
or rigor mortis.
Rooms of conquests.
Rooms of death.

No sign of life
on such heroic scale.
Let's leave.

II
In a side room,
three earth mother figures,
each no taller
than an index finger
hold their bellies
as though - with a laugh -
they could split into twin fruit
like chestnuts.

Side by side
with a child size sarcophagus
stands a small clay bath.

A narrow ornamental ribbon
runs around its rim
following the gentle curves
of its sides
and raised head rest
that's tilted backwards slightly
to accommodate a body

as precisely
as a shoe someone's foot.

2000 years left no mark
on its form.
Its highest function
lying on the scale
of intimacy and touch,
it is compact
and serviceable.

Let's rest
in this room for a while
where the objects are small
and enduring.
Time shrinks all conquests
to nothing,
but everything here
is large as life:

a Boetian woman
in a finely patterned garment,
a bronze cow that can fit
onto a palm,
a tiny child
holding an even tinier goose.

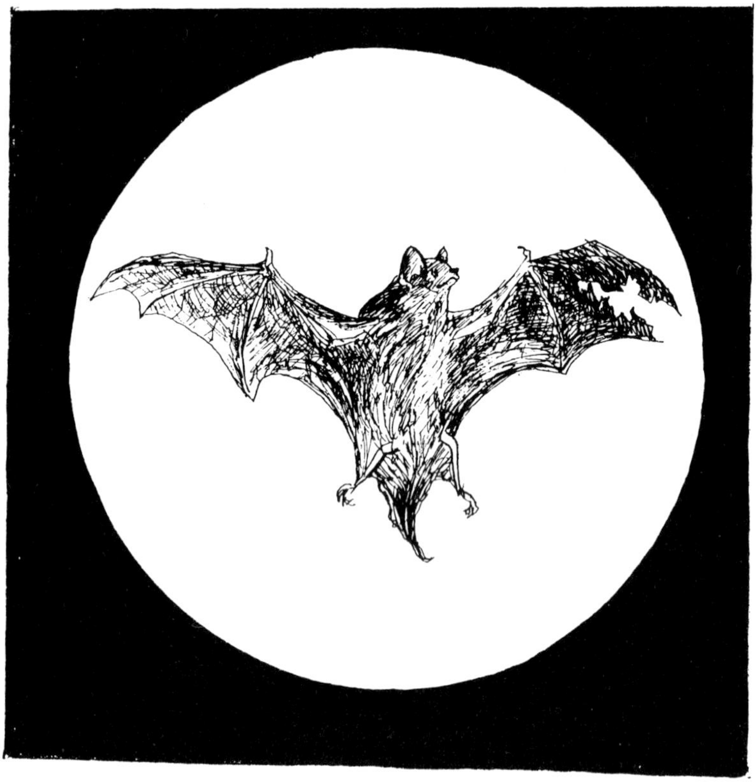

Young Bat

A shred of wrinkled black polythene
blown in through the bathroom window
was at second glance a young bat
clinging to the synthetic fleece
of the floormat.

When I bent down
to its thimbleful of body
its shrivelled ancient man's face,
it bared tiny fangs
and hissed twice
to warn me,
who loomed huge and white above it,
quickly opening and shutting
the half-torn fan
of its spoked wings.

It was about two in the morning,
outside the night was black,
and all its blackness
was repeated
in that ink blot
on the blazing tiles.

Little parachutist,
its radar gone haywire,
crashlanded in the bathroom
where sinks, tubs, mirrors
and steel

conspired to withhold sanctuary,
it lay in the neon glare
fiercely exposed,
ready to take on any Goliath.

Would it ever have guessed
how far I was from harming it,
how I longed to be like it
a fellow traveller of owls
with a close knowledge of territories
echoing beyond top branches
and insect-filled summer nights?

I turned off the lights
and shook the mat gently
out the window
to release its grip,
it let go,
did one crazy loop
and was carried away
on a dark wave.

Litany For The Pig

Sorrowful and pale brother,
sister, sacrificed
countless times,

your name - sullied,
dragged through the mud
for thousands of years -
be praised.

Most generous of all creatures,
you give yourself totally.

Noble pig,
pig undefiled,
pig beloved by many nations,
immaculate pig!

Once you reigned in the chestnut forest,
the closed garden of purity,
in a coat of dark fur,
energy bristling on slim flanks,
wrathful and protective
parent of striped princelings.

Savant and high-priest,
worshipped and devout,
trotting on split hooves
over the tiles of sinking temples

as swiftly
as through the padded grounds
of airy, leafy dominions,

the earth took you
into soft miry arms,
rocked you in warm ponds,
gave up to you only
its black buried wonder,
the rotting velvet of the truffle.

You were mother
of cunning and kindness
when you arrived,
an emissary from great distance,
light as Ariel,
your body the simple curved outline
and firmness
of a water jug,
your white-lashed eyes
full of wit and knowledge
of other worlds.

The word made flesh,
you dwelt among us,
but we closed our ears
to your message.

The deaf president didn't hear,
nor the philosopher of the taverns,

not the soldier,
nor the professor.

And now it's too late.
You were free,
so we crushed you.
We insulted you with our refuse,
you who was used to a diet
of acorn and sage,
chestnut and wild thyme.

You had to become more like us,
naked, exposed, fearful.

Torn limb from limb,
you're no more
than a grotesque swelling fruit,
squashed into stinking prisons
breeding generations of slaves.

Captive, trembling,
and devoured,
silent lamb to the slaughter -
your heart is broken.

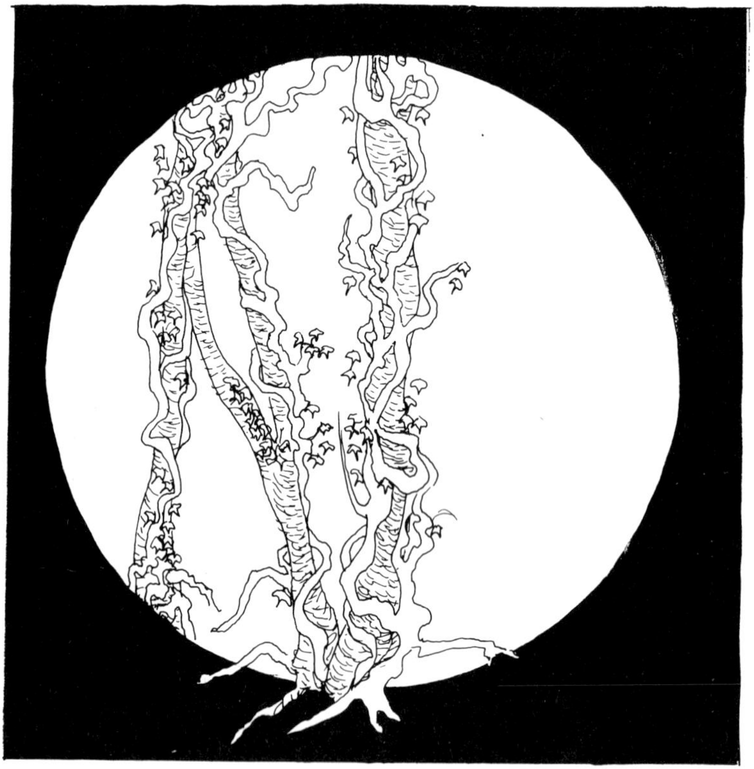

The Elder

I come to the rescue of the elder
that grows at the back of the garden.
The old weatherer of storms,
host of pebble-grey spiders
inside their spun-yard fabrications,
their mock suns,
home of blackbird and thrush,
is dangerously ill.

For several seasons it deceived me
with rich, glossy foliage,
but now I've got wise
to its pernicious Siamese twin,
the common creeping helix, the ivy,
twisting its way up and up
to spread out its own top-heavy evergreen crown.

Though it's almost hopeless
I try to banish this hanger-on,
the sap-sucker growing strong on the elder.
How it turns up wherever you look,
well-armed imperialist, holding the tree
in a wrestler's grip with bearded tendrils,
how it clings and chokes,
to put out its own waxen black berries.

With a sharp blade I attack the parasite,
lop off serpentine growths, pull limb from limb,

lift varicose knots, lay bare
to the daylight the damage:
a wild crop of dead wood,
corrugated bark, powdered with sawdust,
a wrinkled trunk,
desiccated by thousands of hairfine roots.

The elder is sick.
Cool and secretive shadow
in the yards of childhood,
hoisting white flags over country lanes,
I must try to save it
for its saucers full of violet fruit
held out all for the birds,
for the elderflower's pungent cat-smell
on June nights,
its yellowish wood, "pleasantly grained
and very suitable for carvings",
its crimson juices, teas, wines and dishes,
Sambucus Nigra,
famous all the way from here to Siberia.

I continue climbing higher
and higher, dropping branches
below me as I loosen tangles,
open clenched fists,
unravel the ivy's stranglehold.

And the elder begins to breathe more freely,
or so I imagine,

it straightens up, shakes itself
and turns its leaves towards the light
that filters through into its core
for the first time in years,
sends the circulation flying to the top,
and the roots deeper into the ground
where the water is purer.

Chaplin Mimes Mr. Hyde Turning Into Dr. Jekyll

Chaplin alone
on a rose
a pocket watch
a walking stick
a tight rope
in one pair of galoshes
plus two oversize patent leather boots.

Forget your everlasting laundry bills,
ladies and gentlemen,
the transformation is about to begin.

Note the fringes of doves
the absence of safety nets
or other implements
as the claws come off.
Three cheers for the claws!

The pocket watch says 3 seconds to 12.
The doctor is meticulous
in his habits.

Paulette comes in on tiptoe
blowing kisses in the face
of all this hair falling in fistfuls.

The famous teeth

chased by a snarl around the ring
are caught in the great drum
where they rumble and thunder.

Is it for my amusement,
ladies and gentlemen,
that you grow carnations all over?

The director and the chief clerk
are having sherbet with a star.
Boxing champs jitterbug
with sad Jewish barbers.
Policemen on the wing fill the tent.

This is the age of innocence
in our city of the angels.
It will bring the house down
with confetti
or your money back.

Chaplin meanwhile alone
on fringes of doves
a tightrope
a walking stick
a pocket watch
a rose.
Above a chalk-white mouth
a small black moustache
rises up
in panic.

Voltaire's Monkeys

How tiresome this business of love
and its pitiful claim
on the entire world's attention!

Pat loves Edel

We who have our eyes everywhere
see with distaste
how love spreads nightly
on walls and fences like weeds.

Martina loves Paul

It would be laughable
in the face of our moral authority

Philemon loves Baucis

if we hadn't failed in controlling
a single butterfly's lust,

Dante loves Beatrice

unfortunately the fishes and crabs
on the bottom of rivers and seas
are way out of earshot

Mary loves Joseph

and the trees tend to have
such a forceful leaning towards each other.
See how shamelessly they caress every breeze
with thousands of fingers!

David loves Jonathan

Even the crows sit very close together
on the budding branches
we can only guess
what they are up to up there

Romeo loves Juliet

and the proximity of stone to stone
is more than we can bear.

What else can we do but turn our backs
on all those disgusting signs
of the magnetism of the flesh

and like Voltaire
hold four monkeys in captivity
and mistreat them daily
with sermons and speeches.

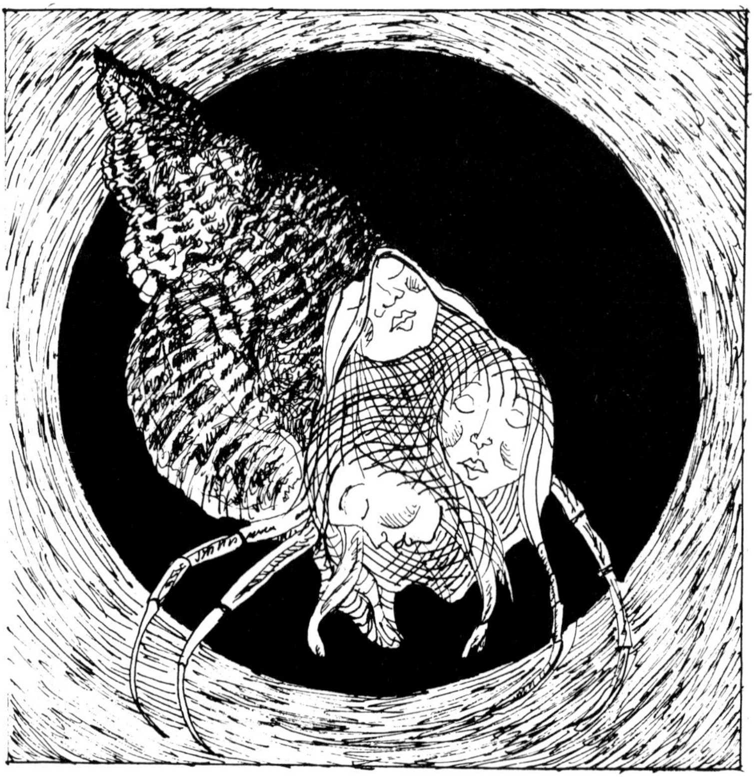

Sea Escape

Miriam, child of fifteen, going to sleep
retreats into her room
like a hermit crab into its shell,

and dreams, carried downstream
towards a bay

that is neither here nor there
with its quicksand beaches
and wandering strands.

Paint brushes on her worktable
cloud a water jar blue.

The sea she's just given a touch
of aquamarine

is filled to the brim with life.

Moving back and forth on the coast
of her sleep

it holds its one long deep note
like the bow of a double bass,

beats a kettledrum
to the tune of dolphin and whale,

it's a glass bowl
splintering against the rocks,

a pillow of smelling salts;

at eventide
its cities of foam and ice
tower above Manhattan,

lit up by ribbons and ribbons
of phosphorescent fishes;

it plays cowboys and Indians
taking arrow after arrow
from its quiver of gales,

it is a silent black animal
coming up to her knee to be stroked.

In the morning,
just before she awakes,

she finds on the floorboards
a jellied stalk full of green bubbles,
a starfish like a small suction dredge,

an ink-coloured squid
throwing open all its arms.

Diptych Of A Wedding

An early spring day.
There's a touch of winter
still in the air,
but the wind coming from the plains
already smells of orchards.
I'm on my own, the others having gone
to vineyards and fields.

I dawdle in the courtyard,
although I know the new commission
must be ready by the month,
then cross over to the garden,
to my bed of healing plants.
"Take care", my father often says in jest,
"that one day they don't burn you at the stake!"

I know I'm stalling, but the work
holds no attraction for me
on a day like this,
the rows of portraits in the studio,
deadpan princes, courtesans,
councillors.
I do them to perfection,
not with love but skill,
painting for my keep
under my father's or brother's name.

I dig the earth up for a while
where winter rains laid bare some roots,
then straighten up and go back
to the workshop
which is lit by windows facing north.
I contemplate my choice of colours and begin.

A diptych of a wedding.
The party's over, all the guests have gone.
The couple's sitting in a bath.
His hair is tied back, her face is pale.
They can't be older than sixteen,
the usual match
made by her dowry, his name.

The other panel is of the bedroom;
the two are lying still
between the sheets.
A dark brown bedspread, terra-cotta tiles,
an armchair carved from ebony.

In the background
there's the portrait of myself
dressed as a servant woman
in white apron and frilled cap.

Quietly I shuffle around
and straighten cushions, blankets,
place a water jug upon a table
and finally untie a curtain
to let it fall across the bed.

Consolation
for Gabriel

At times everyone's worried thought
must turn to the primeval slime
for consolation and future confidence,
away from reports of overkill
through the bomb,
of nerve gas in leaking containers
or clouds of biological annihilation
blowing across the Atlantic,
all the doomsday varieties
and features of blithe self-destruction
gathering as mutated smiles
in genetically impossible mouth corners,
as senile generals play war games
in a sandbox.

For that is the great moment of the amoeba:
joining forces to glob-of-spit size,
they pull in their pseudo-feet
and await the terrestial blitz
and the final ice-cold whimper,
their protoplasmic memory banks
programmed to contain data
on murky pools and saltwater puddles,
their self-indulgent empire,
after the curtain has dropped
on the nuclear stage.
Assuming new shapes endlessly,

they give themselves to division,
re-division and growth
and brainless dreams
of single cell dominion
until, through a quirky chemical kick-off,
the ball of evolution
starts rolling again.

Orpheus And Eurydice
In The Underground

Everything revolves around Eros
above on Piccadilly or elsewhere,
as distantly smiling, black uniformed men
point me towards metal stairs
that lower me fast
into the vaulted corridors of the Underground,
where a gigantic panting sewing machine
stitches the vast underskirts of the city together
with swiftly moving needles.

Heading towards Bakerloo
I am suddenly swept aside head over heels
into the wake of a rapidly floating group of deaf mutes,
engaged in silent discussion,

a ping pong match of words
which they roll between their palms
to toss them lightly to each other,
they pull them from their sleeves
and send them fluttering to the ceiling,
pluck images from thin air,
puns from subterranean trees full of fruit,
they pick double entendres
from each others' chins and noses
in an eloquent game of throw-away phrase
and catching of joke.

The cause of all this excitement
seems to be a young couple
walking in the middle of the group,
oblivious of the tumult around them.
The girl, her head on his shoulder,
passes word after speechless word to him
who eats from her hand -
Orpheus and Eurydice ascending together,
dumbfounded by love.

I watch them as they are carried along by the others
away from the tunnelled dark,
and know that when they reach the stairs,
this time there will be no looking back.

Gertrud Kolmar, 1894 - 1943

Among thousands of grey faces,
among thousands of grey shadows
silently crossing the threshold
into the chambers of death,
I see her,
Gertrud Kolmar,
poet from Berlin,
deported in 1943,
all trace of her lost since then.

Her flowers, her day - and animal - dreams,
her yearned-for child,
her poems -
ashes in the grates of Auschwitz.

Gertrud Kolmar,
child princess playing
with a small blue heart
she'd plucked from a tree in her garden
where the changeling toad hopped
on spotted legs,
the salamander told its tale
of ice and fire.
Night and day
she prepared for the child:
a spinning-top sun,
a waffle moon
and the earth a strawberry hill

tumbling with foam.
A stuffed seal dreamt of a ship
with a rag of sky nailed to its mast.

Gertrud Kolmar
turned down all chances of escape,
determined to share her people's fate:
the stake, screws, gallows, rack
and finally the deadly gas
in the chambers of Auschwitz.

As the days drew colder
she wrapped herself in solitude,
her warmest cloak,
or wore the dress of green silk
in which she longed to be mother,
witch or child snatcher.
Well aware of the danger
she wrote of large birds with wrinkled necks
that hovered close
in the crumbling brickwork,
wishing to be a wave
breaking on a distant shore.

Gertrud Kolmar,
lost in the anonymity
of the deathcamps,
the digits of annihilation
burnt into her flesh,

*entered the 'towers of death
encircled by demon vultures,'*

*wilted song, extinguished script
followed the bitter call,
died silently,
the eternal sigh
devoured by the howling wind.*

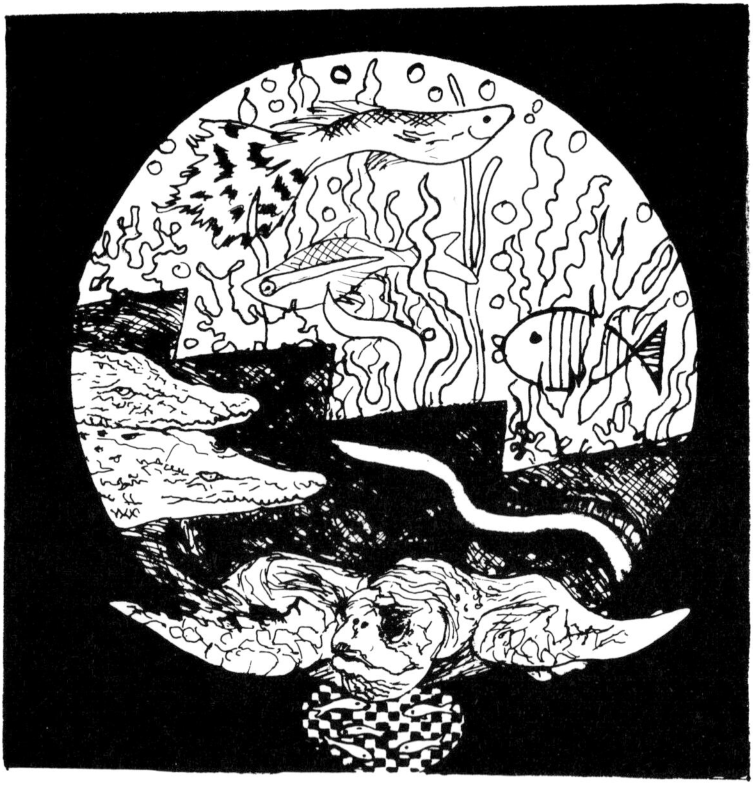

The Aquarium
for Benji

If you ever visit the aquarium
with its wall panelling of fish tanks
full of sweet-water fishes
and exotic fishes from Africa
or the Caribbean,
little transparent ones
that have swallowed
tiny
neon lights,
some with dashes and spots
like tigerlilies trailing petal-shaped tails,

some in such colours and stripes
they must have been painted by children and
come to life in the water,
some that are wrapped in grandmother's best mantilla,
some warriors in armour of scales,
bearded,
spiked,
with sharp teeth
and razorblade fin span,
some that float
sideways
and some with their mouths agape
on their backs,

and if you should get tired of all this
as it sways in the bubbling tanks
and rises and sinks and goggles dumbly,
darts up and drifts
through the feathery leaves
of underwater ferns
in endless motion,
then sneak away
and
    tip
        toe
            down
                the
                    blue-
                        tiled
                            stairs,

past
the knobbly turquoise china Neptune,
past
potted palmtrees and creeping Lianas,
down into
the twi
light
of the cellars,
into the green half-light
seeping from the glass walls,
the emerald glow of an old forgotten laboratory.

Here is neither day nor night,
but permanent
gloom.
The things lurking darkly behind the panes
are very old.
Walk past the alligators lying in a heap on each other,
a silent pile of grey logs,
past the savage moray uncoiling its black body
to raise its head and fix you
with slanting phosphorous eyes,
past the electric eel,
its voltage harnessed and crackling softly,
until you come to the
GIANT TURTLE
the oldest inmate of this city.

Look respectfully at the
curve
of its vulture-neck,
its bird's-of-prey beak,
how it surfaces to breathe very rarely
dragging long shreds of parchment skin in the murky water.
Time has stopped
before the glass wall of its tank.
Everything happened while it revolved
slowly,
staring at the changing crowds
with unblinking reptilian
eyes:

there were shouts of
'Long Live the King',
'Down with the Tyrant',
the thumping of military boots,
the strains of dance music,
hurrahs and screams,
the ratatat of guns,
the drums of war,
the songs of peace-times.

If you stand here
for a while,
you can
feel
how
ab
so
lute
ly

still

everything

is.

Set into the wall on one side
is a circular basin in jade and purple mosaics,
where five goldfish
hang
motionlessly

in the
...water...
Their bodies have lost all metallic shine
in the eternal dusk.
Throw in a penny for luck!
It glints at the bottom,

a small circle of light...

The Book

The pages of this book breathe
and extend and open up
with the slowness of seasons,
its covers grow forests
of roots in your hands,
its heartbeats advance and recede
like the waves of the sea.

It draws its pulse, its music,
from the rush of water over rocks,
and once in a while,
as you turn the pages,
a bird flashes past,
a fish leaps up above the surface.

Read the fine blue lines
of its blood vessels
the words dropping one by one
gently as fruit from its branches,
the letters
sequined with dozens of flies.

Watch the moon in its circle of clouds
or the midday sun
pass in the book's mirror,
and the stars and planets
illuminate its script.

Best of all,
read while you're asleep
under trees,
listening to their wind organs.
Read carefully to the end,
letting the words build nests
among the leaves of your dream.

The Breakthrough

The latest discovery -
the latest truth -
calculations,
chronicles.

Very small piles of feathers,
a few mandibles,
bones, fossils,
gauze rags

bring to light:
place of birth -
elsewhere
date of birth -
another time.

What can be gathered
from lines scratched
into eggshells,
from sudden changes
in the direction of birdflight
or clouds?

Mountains arise in waves of rock
across a plain;
a lake replaces the desert.

(In the graticules
lines rise and sink
from heresiarch to saint,
reason to soul,
fire to thirst.)

It's guesswork from now on:
genuflection or curse,
slaughter or transfiguration.
Who knows, in the absence
of papyrus or ink?

Verifiable only
the graptolitic evidence -
handprints on cave walls,
human shapes
blitzed onto buildings,
faces like scripted stone,
fissured, lacerated,

buried between laminae of shale.

Day Return, Suffolk, Summer '86
for Mary

We travelled backwards on our journey
to the sea, the Royal Rails
narrowed, we rested on upright blue
cushions. Almost curtseying
the conductor handed back tickets, we fancied
that people already wore unfamiliar dress,
hats, belts, buttons of past fashions
showing the mark of a different,
more fastidious standard of artistry.
With glass-beaded fringes, nails painted
sea green, black women appeared as mermaids,
others had the fine point
of their hairlines shaved, the dome
of their foreheads a bleached white oval,
just perfect, so it seemed,
for miniature portraits, medallions.
The sun flew past on hedges, wheatfields,
enlivened by earth-moving moles,
magpies taking things in their stride,
past on red-brick villages in rings
of poplars, where swallows hightailed it
through gauze screens of small black flies.
We had our backs to the sea throughout
but felt the breeze cooling,
saw the grass acquire
the sharper knife-edge of sea grass.

On the platform our heads were turned instantly
by two sisters who brought us to the wilderness
of their garden, dined us on raspberries, wine,
took us to where the sea had swallowed
a city. Daily wet-suited frogmen
floated through sunken submarine streets
shaded by sea plants,
desirously swished round shell-covered spires,
moreover an abbey had to be carried
stone by stone backwards
from treacherous sandcliffs, they said,
buying flounders poundwise
straight from the boat.
They gave us sea-punctured hagstones
to ward off evil, found cornelians
tinted deep red by the water.
Sizewell Nuclear Plant rose in the distance,
squat and malignant as a warship.
We watched a long-tailed kite
unfurl its astonishing series of stunts
before this menacing backdrop.
It looped and spiralled higher
and higher until it vanished
through a minute hole in the sky.

The Butcher
for Rita

He's retired now
and runs a dogs' home.
In his heyday as butcher
he was an artist

although not many appreciated
his dexterity,
his savoir faire
with flesh and blood.

His discerning eye
and steady touch
made his butcher shop window
a rare thing

that served beauty
and no other interest.
The piquancy of colour,
vibrant, understated,

transcended the material
and went straight
to the heart
of suffering.

Where others saw nothing
but skin, muscle, bone,

he saw a universe
pulsating with pigments,

himself as creator
at its dead centre:
Two stuffed pheasants
stand below garlands

of plastic grapes.
A mandarin drake
struts through autumn leaves
on the other side.

The sheep lying on display
like the centrepiece
of a crucifixion
has the pale circle of its neck

wrapped carefully
in a paper ruche.
Its front legs
hold a green apple.

Pygmalion

She's always at a loss for words for him
nor could she follow him
down the garden paths
of his homemade labyrinth
of word games.
He reasons with stones,
granite, slabs of bedrock,
then summons his fifty summers
to flower in the thinning strata
of her resistance,
her lazy-beds.

His head vacillates majestically
between breaths of hot air
and the still authority
of carved rock.
The chips sink and glide,
multi-layered, cool as silk.
In his workshop marble is textured,
a fabric with tassels.
That suits him fine.
And wanting to flatter her, to win her,
he chisels arrangements at her feet
of full-blown poppies,
their seed capsules erect
and bursting with black sand
into their wrinkled paper handkerchiefs.

What keeps her inside
this hedged-in neighbourhood garden
hoodwinked into an unequal match?
His mesmeric tools?
His line-up of stone narcissi
behind their palisades,
the blood-wild gladiolus spears,
the grip and throttle
of convulvulus?

Speechlessly she passes his muster
and vantage point
to spread the muslin of her lapidary soul
between the webbed silences
of gadfly and noxious fungi,
fever speckled and crimson,
and unobserved at last
her flesh and bones
withdraw into the centre of stone,
unhewn and blackened with moss.

But when the afternoon fires
itself into lulls he comes
with his chisel to rub out her wrong ways.
her imperfections, and moaning,
she takes up position,
his cars cocked like two sentries
for thunder and lightning to strike
a resemblance of saved face.

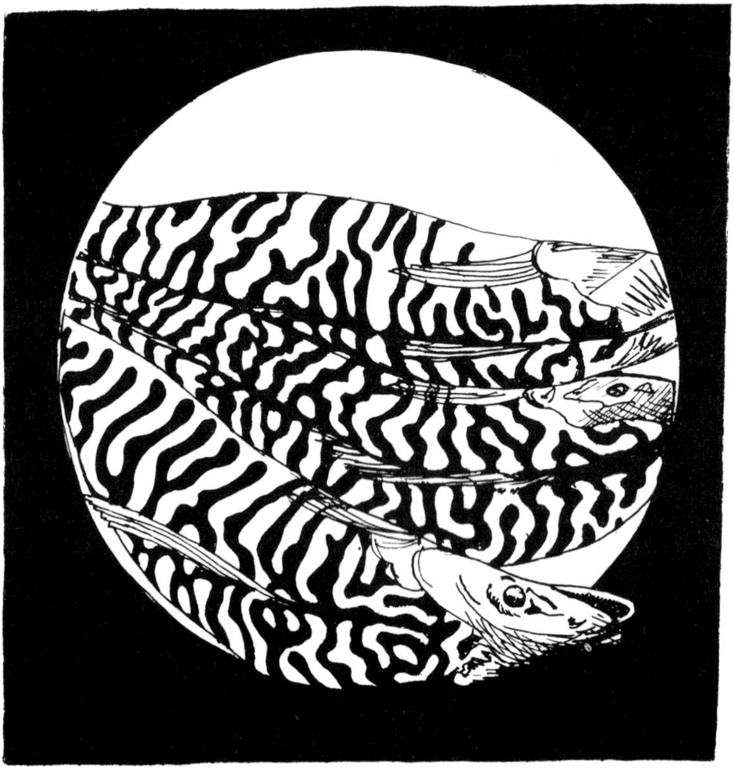

Mackerel

Shoals of mackerel out before the coastline
Fishing trawlers have an easy picking
Fishes stroll into the nets unbidden
Head and shoulders first into the meshwork
Sure as tightrope walkers on the rope.

Midnight and the fleet lies in the harbour.
Cut-price in such multitude the mackerel
Slide into the boxes, forklift drivers
Do not waste a moment while unloading,
Do not gather what spills on the jetty,

Twitches, flounders, rolling in their hundreds,
Gaping-mouthed with tinsel-shiny bodies
On the oil-smeared tarmac, swiftly they are
Picked up by a single file of after-
Hours carousers from the bars, some lucky

Down-and-outs and in among them also
Quiet-spoken family men, into the
Plastic bags and sheets of newsprint wander
Mackerel, seafresh, salty and delicious
For the breakfast over many flames.

Quick at home you slit and gut the fishes,
Roe, intestines, bladders in the cat-dish,
Twenty, thirty inches long such marvels
Sizzle in the roundness of the pan.
Oil and garlic, twig of thyme and bayleaf

Give a taste so tender you'll turn colour,
An aroma of the wild blue ocean
That you dream of octopus and coral

And the legendary floating islands
Where the happy people are forever
Playing ball with jellyfish and sharks.

Adolescence

Two young sisters cartwheel across the grass
beside a small cold lake
which is so entirely ringed by mountains
we can only see a pale, dish-shaped segment of sky.
A stone rises in the mild, slightly chilly autumn air,
spiders climb slopes of evening light,
high pitched children's voices carry across to us
from somewhere between the trees.

The girls grip the ground for a split second
with both hands and spin around,
then let fly again and again,
as though they never quite touched down
on the darkening field,
or a simple trick could make them float
to the pine tops, levitate, walk on water.
One lost a sneaker, the other's ponytail came undone.

Fallen angels,
keep them from stumbling,
from the slow, overpowering pull of the earth;
let the sun be their ferris wheel
above a vast fairground
carrying the blue circles of days
the green circles of water and trees
into the night and out again.